Love so romantic

A passionate Love

Mia Lily

Table of Contents

Chapter 1

The Gathering

This facility, known as the miracle clinic, is located in Liang state.

The reason for the clinic's name is that everyone who is brought there unwell would instantly recover. Dr. Ru Ying, a well-known physician known for his mischievous and humorous nature, owns and runs the clinic. At the end of each month, he distributes number cards to those who are ill.

Knowing this, the ill often congregate at the clinic's entrance, amid Themis. Si Xiaowan, whose brother is wheelchair-bound as a result of an accident he experienced while gathering herbs on a cliff.

Su Xiaovwan, who is known for being stubborn, pretended to be sick so that she could meet the doctor herself to collect a number card, vomiting fake blood so that she could enter the clinic. She saw this as an opportunity to help her brother regain his mobility, so she joined the crowd to collect number cards so she could enter the clinic. Unfortunately, it finished when it was her turn.

Gu yanxi, the young master of the Gu mansion, walks into the house at the same moment and witnesses everything that is happening at the front of the clinic as all the females inside are swooning over him. He is the most amazing, kind, hardworking, and handsome young guy.

Su Xiaowan decided to remain calm, but she made the mistake of kicking Gu Yanxi at his when she was being taken to the clinic. The young master immediately realized she was lying and stopped the people from taking her in. He said he could treat her. Upon seeing this, Su Xiaowan spit out another blood because she was afraid of the pin. Upon realizing her plan had succeeded, she grinned contentedly.

When she met with the doctor, she lied repeatedly, but the doctor realized it and decided to go along with it. She convinced

Dr. Ru to give her a number card, and when Ru asked her name, she wrote down her brother's name, "Su Xiaoan." She then left happily, but not for long because she ran into Gu Yanxi, who called her a cheater in front of everyone at the clinic. Luckily, she managed to escape.

When she got home, she was overjoyed and told Xiaoan everything, but when she went to give Xiaoan the number card, she couldn't find it. Then, as she replayed everything that had happened while Yanxi was holding her hand at the clinic's entrance, she yelled in her head, "uhhhhh GU YANXI," "how dare he steals my hard-earned card!" She crept inside the Gu house at night just as someone broke through the gate; at first, she was terrified but later realized he was coming for the same mission known as "OPERATION TAKING WHAT IS MINE." She then asks the man, "Where is Gu Yanxi's room?" After he showed her the route, they arrive at his door.

Chapter 2

"Recovering what is mine

After successfully searching the room for the number card, but being unable to locate it, she crept inside the room while making no noise and peered through the door to hear someone taking a bath. Xiaowan saw the material Yanxi was wearing and thought about seeing through it, but she didn't know how, so she chose to skulk into the restroom. She promptly located the card, which made her extremely pleased. As she turned to go, she made the dumb error of treading on the cloth, which caused it to fall and make a sound. Gu yànxi then said, "Is that you, Shi Sheng (his guard), can you kindly bring my cloth and belt?" When Yànxi said, "What about my belt?" Xiaowan turned around and placed the belt on him before lowering her head to tie the knot of the belt. She had opted to dress for him since he was turning his back. In response,

Xiaowan grinned and said, "I'm here to take what is mine because I don't quickly realize someone of a rich standard like the Gu's family can take what is mine ohhh." Yanxi opened his mouth to respond, "don't worry since I have what is mine I'll be fine. " However, he was unable to. He quickly collected his belt and turned around. "you, what do you think you are doing," he said

She immediately departed. Where have you been before that monster entered, Shi Sheng said, clutching his forehead, "Young master, are you alright?" I believed it was a thief, so I said, "Master, what monster are you talking about?" "Go get that little thief, and bring her here alive," was the answer.

As for Xiaowan, she was attempting to flee but it seemed that all of the mansion's guards had been dispatched. However, as soon as she turned around, she saw another man who claimed to be here for the same purpose. "They are so many how will I walk out uhh," she muttered with a disappointed look.

"It's alright, I'm well known in this house," he said. Xiaowan wasn't sure whether to trust him or not, but the guards observed them cuddling and took no action since the guy was Gu Ziqian, the second young master of Gu's home.

He assisted Xiaowan in escaping the mansion, while Gu Yanxi, who was enraged, decided to control her anger since they were unable to locate her.

Chapter 3

"Getting what is mine back"

She managed to enter the room quietly and after unsuccessfully looking around for the number card, she heard someone taking a bath and peered through the door. Yanxi's cloth drew Xiaowan's attention, and she thought about seeing through it. Unsure of how Xiaowan chose to enter the restroom covertly. Fortunately, she arrived at the location of the cloth. She quickly searched for the number card and discovered it, which made her very happy. As she turned to leave, however, she made the silly mistake of stepping on the cloth, which caused it to fall and make a sound. Gu yànxi then asked, "Is that you, Shi Sheng (his guard), can you please bring my cloth and belt?" After dressing him since he was turning his back, Xiaowan started to go but Yànxi interrupted, asking, "What about my belt?" She then went back and placed the belt on him and dipped her head to tie the knot. In response, Xiaowan grinned and said, "I'm here to take what is mine because I don't quickly realize someone of a rich standard like the Gu's family can take what is mine ohhh." Yanxi opened his mouth to respond, "don't worry since I have what is mine I'm fine," but was unable to. "don't worry since I have what is mine I'm fine," he said, turning around.

She departed right away. Young Master, are you okay? Where have you been before that monster came in, Shi Sheng said as she entered, patting his forehead. Go catch the tiny thief and bring her here alive. "Master what monster are you talking about? I thought it was a thief." "Yes, sir."

As for Xiaowan, she was attempting to flee but it appeared that all of the mansion's guards had been dispatched. However, as soon as she turned around, she encountered another man who claimed to be here for the same purpose. "They are so many how will I

go out uhh," she said with a defeated expression.
Xiaowan wasn't sure whether to trust him when he said, "it's alright, I'm well known in this house," but before she could decide, the guards saw them embracing, so no action was taken since the guy is Gu Ziqian, the second young master of Gu's home.
In contrast, Gu yànxi, who was enraged, decided to cool down since they couldn't locate Xiaowan. He assisted Xiaowan in escaping the house.

Chapter 4

Gu Wan'er (1) regaining what is rightfully mine

After trying in vain to find the number card, she was able to enter the room without being noticed. Hearing someone having a bath, she then looked through the door. Xiaowan saw Yanxi's garment and wondered whether she could see through it. Xiaowan opted to sneak inside the bathroom since she wasn't sure how. Thankfully, she made it to where the cloth was. She instantly looked around for the number card and was delighted to find it. However, she foolishly stepped on the fabric as she turned to walk away, causing it to fall and create a sound. "Is that you, Shi Sheng (his guard), could you kindly bring my cloth and belt?" Gu yànxi enquired. When Xiaowan finished clothing him because he was turning his back, Yànxi interrupted and said, "What about my belt?" After that, she walked back and put the belt on him before lowering her head to make a knot. "I'm here to take what is mine because I don't fast comprehend someone of a wealthy standard like the Gu's family can steal what is mine ohhh," Xiaowan said with a smile. Don't worry because I have what is mine, I'm OK, Yanxi tried to say, but he was unable to. Don't worry, I'm OK, he added, turning around. "I have what is mine.

She immediately departed. You alright, Young Master? Shi Sheng tapped his forehead as she arrived and said, "Where have you been before that monster came in." Bring the little thief here alive if you capture her. "What creature are you referring to, Master? I assumed it was a thief." I agree, sir.

Xiaowan was making an effort to run, but it seemed that all of the mansion's guards had been called off duty. But as soon as she turned back, another guy appeared who said he was coming for the same reason. She added, looking disheartened, "They are so many, how will I walk out?

When he said, "I'm well known in this house," Xiaowan wasn't sure whether to believe him, but before she could make up her mind, the guards observed them kissing, and because the man was Gu Ziqian, the second young master of Gu's household, no action was taken.

Gu yànxi, who was furious, chose to remain calm since they were unable to find Xiaowan. He helped Xiaowan leave the home.

Chapter 5

With jewelry in her hair and a haircut that was crafted exactly for her. Gu yànxi pondered whether she may be more beautiful than the actual Gu Wan'er. Gu yànxi instructed Xiaowan to behave by Grandma's instructions and to make up tales on her own as they made their way to her courtyard. Xiaowan agreed, thinking, "another opportunity to bring him down."

After reaching the courtyard, they went into grandma's chamber, where she was ecstatic to see Gu Wan'er. Grandma: "Wan'er, my darling, where have you been just look at you, so slender and bony, who took care of you?" "She exclaimed, giving her a strong embrace.

"Lagoon is so happy, thank yànxi for bringing Wan'er back," grandma said, "grandma it's nothing, and thank goodness little sister is back. They were about to leave when grandma said, "yànxi please protect and take care of your little sister. I can't afford to lose her again "Yanxi nodded and committed.

Xiaowan nods to begin her duties as Gu yànxi's maid after Gu yànxi reminds her of her job as she exits the building.

After spending some time at the mansion and assuming the identity of Gu Wan'er Xiaowan becomes used to her circumstances and begs Gu yànxi for permission once she finishes her daily tasks, but yànxi likes tormenting her every day.

Despite all of Gu yánxi's insults directed at her, he seems to find himself pleased and enamored by her naughty behaviors, such as chatting excessively.

After living in the Gu family mansion for a while, she finally realized one night that she was only there for her brother and brother A'ye. To find him, she searched the entire property but was unsuccessful. Just as she had given up hope of finding him, she felt someone touch her face. Turning around, she saw the person she had been searching for all day, with a smiling face. Gu Ziqian

asked, "Are you looking for me?," to which she responded, "Of course, where have you been all day." He searched his memory for a good lie, and eventually came up with the one that went like this: "Actually, you know I work here, so I am a personal guard to the second master of this mansion, and I escort him somewhere far uh." He snapped his fingers together to break her out of her daze, "Ohh sorry you said..?", but he was at a loss for words as he wondered what she was contemplating. He turned to leave, but Xiaowan grabbed him and said, "Brother Aye have you forgotten me, don't you remember me, I gave this jade back to you when we were young," with a hopeful expression, believing that he couldn't possibly have forgotten her. Not at all.
When she lost hope of finding him, she felt someone cover her face. Turning around, she saw the person she had been searching for all day. Rather than responding to her, Gu Ziqian stared at the jade that remembered him. She searched the mansion

but couldn't find him. When she lost hope, she felt someone cover her face. Turning around, she saw the person she had been searching for all day. He snapped his fingers together to break her out of her daze, "oh sorry you said...?", but he was at a loss for words as he wondered what she was contemplating. As he turned to leave, Xiaowan grabbed him and asked, "Brother Aye have you forgotten me, don't you remember me, I gave this jade back to you when we were young." She said with a hopeful expression, thinking he couldn't possibly have forgotten, Not at all.

Gu Zi Qian's elder brother Gu yànxi handed him the jade bead since yànxi had lost his memory as a result of the accident when he fell from the cliff, so instead of responding, Gu ziqian just gazed at it. When Zicqian realized that the person she was referring to as his brother A'ye was Gu yànxi rather than him, he chose to go along with her. Zicqian lifted his head, assuming that this woman had something to do with his brother. He said, "uhh, I can't recall anybody from my childhood past and I'm sorry, so what is your name," and Xiaowan, who had been in love with him all year, was ready to start crying, stammered out, "Su... Xiaowan."

Chapter 6

Memories from the past

She stumbled, "Su... Xiaowan." "Ohhhh Xiaowan, that's wonderful, how about we meet here daily, uhh at least you will help me get some memories back about our childhood past, how about that?" he smiled. She immediately agreed, and Gu ziqian walked away, leaving her there.

She replied, grinning and muttering to herself, "Yes, yes, yes hurray brother Aye, I will make sure you remember everything and never forget me again." She had no idea that someone was observing her.

When she arrived at the mansion and saw him gazing at the flowers in the garden, she called out to him, "brother Aaye." Hearing this familiar voice, he turned around to see Xiaowan pointing out potatoes to him. He collected one and stared at it, then she said, "brother A'ye you love to eat."

Gu Ziqian smiled upon seeing his brother, asking Gu yànxi, who had been staring at the two since he emerged to speak with him, "Anything funny that you are smiling, uhh, and what is that black thing in your hand anyway?" "Ziqian smiled in response to his disgust at the color, saying, "Oh, this is potato, smoked potatoes, uh, it's black outside but yellow inside see." He tore the potatoes in half so that Yánxi could see what he was talking about. Yánxi nodded his head and stared at it. "Don't just stare like that, come on have some," he said, pointing at the other half. However, Yánxi turned away and left the garden. "Hey brother, it's not like you haven't tasted it before, uhh," ziqian said, looking at the cold brother

When Yànxi invited Xiaowan into his courtyard after she had finished feeding the grandmother, he stated, "Seems like you are free today therefore I've discovered a wonderful job for you instead of wandering about the house all day" He said, "Young Master, what did you want me to do?" with a

stern expression and a frigid tone. She responded with little curiosity since she felt she could accomplish anything, Xiaowan believed someone had smacked her on the head when he said, "Reorganize, my library here, and reset the books in their classified titles. Young Master, can't I do anything else other than arranging books? ", she remarked while pointing to the library. "Why, can't you read and write?"
He responded, viewing this as a chance to keep her away from Ziqian for the whole day since he did not like how close they were becoming every day. "So can you start working, and enough talking," said Xiaowan as she continued to set the book. Whenever she was incorrect, Yànxi would correct her. Until she fell asleep on the book, Yànxi couldn't help but stare at her. Somehow, this girl had intrigued him. He smiled but later acted properly when he saw some saliva coming out of Xiaowan's mouth. He removed the bok immediately and later covered her with

Chapter 7

Jealousy & Friendship

After a while, Xiaowan grew close to Gu Ziqian, whom she mistakenly identified as her brother Aaye, but the closer they grew, the more envious and selfish Gu Yànxi became, refusing to let her leave the mansion except to see Grandma. Xiaowan, who couldn't stand this kind of strict behavior, responded, "I can't do such a thing, young master," to which he sternly Gu yànxi groaned in despair as she says, "Fine, fine, fine you will remain," and then she smiles and exits the courtyard.

In the evening, Xiaowan went to the garden in search of her brother Aaye. Fortunately, he was there when she arrived, looking at something in his hand. Oh, it's nothing, he answered, grinning. Ziqian: mind if we go out today? Let's meet up in the evening since I have to accompany the second young master someplace this morning, alright?

"Sure, no issue," Gu yànxi was enraged to learn that she intended to go out with Ziqian today, so he devised a scheme.
"Young master you called for me" hmm" he replied nodding, "I want to go and pray in the temple today so I want you to follow me there." Xiaowan did not know what to say, she just had to comply or else this cold man would irritate her again. "ok I'll go," she replied. Yanxi was very amused by her answer, he wanted to ask her that is she not planning to go out with Ziqian today but he
Yànxi was getting ready to go when Xiaowan returned. He had been waiting for him inside the carriage, but because he knew she had gone to look for Ziqian, he didn't want to worry her.
Before they reached the shrine, the carriage was completely silent.
Gu yànxi entered, kneeled, and prayed for his grandmother's health. Xiaowan, who was watching everything, also prayed, saying, "Dear Buddha, please help me retrieve brother A'ye's lost memory." Gu

yànxi moaned in despair as he thought, "Is this how much she loved Ziqian?"
After spending some time at the temple and seeing that it is now afternoon, Xiaowan decides that she should just forget about the date for the evening as it would be a lengthy drive to the Gu house.
They reached the middle of the road on their journey, but the horse lost balance due to something that had pierced its skin. In the carriage, Xiaowan was already on top of Yanxi, and the two of them were mistakenly locked in a kiss. The two were in a daze until the carriage driver said, "I'm sorry, young master, but we can't continue our journey."
Xiaowan noticed this and later got the message, but before she could say a word, an arrow was shot in the air beside Xiaowan. Yanxi immediately took her hand and ran into the nearby forest. This was all part of Yanxi's plan because he was trying to lure out his enemies who had planned to ambush him on his way back home from the temple.

Xiaowan glared at yànxi and muttered, "exactly this is it."

- Before they could turn to the other side of the forest and fall into a large hole on top of each other and pass out, these adversaries began sprinting after them but were unable to catch up.

Chapter 8

Disappointed

After capturing the adversaries, Yanxi's guard went out to hunt for him but was unsuccessful. He yelled out to him across the jungle but saw no trace of him. It is now dusk.

Went to the village and waited for Xiaowan as he had agreed to do in front of the shop selling melon seeds, but he saw no sign of her. After waiting all night, he finally gave up and bought some melon seeds and a teddy bear for her. Thinking that she didn't show up because she had a lot to do, he then went to the mansion. When he arrived at the mansion, he was unable to locate her. However, before he could continue looking for her, his guard spotted him and informed him of everything Xiaowan had said. Thinking that Xiaowan was referring to Ziqian, he had a second thought and asked the guard when had they been out and had not yet returned. The guard then suggested that perhaps they were in danger.

As for yànxi and Xiaowan, who are in danger and trapped in the large hole, they both woke up to find each other hugging, but yànxi was so cold that he swatted her hands away. "hmm young master what happened," Xiaowan asked, rubbing her forehead with her palm. yànxi just stared at him icily and said, "seems you are blind enough not to see

She asked her employer, "Young master, are you sure he would find us here? since I fear we took the incorrect way," but there was no response. Instead, Yànxi told her to "shut up," adding, "Fine, but could you join me in calling out for help?" She asked him to do something that Yànxi believed was silly, but he subsequently accepted and yelled "help! help! help." They sat down to relax a while knowing that no one could locate them when Xiaowan suddenly spoke, "Young master, I have an idea." "How about you hoist me up, so if I get out I will go search for someone to assist or I will help you out too, so what do you think?" yànxi gesticulated as she peered at her with curiosity. She attempted to say something positive, but Yànxi just gave her a stern look as if he should chastise her into submission. Instead, he took into account the circumstances at hand and said, "Why would you walk on my back? I am your master; I should tread on your back." This comment surprised Xiaowan, but she merely nodded, continuing their plan. However, Xiaowan spent a lot of time making excuses to Yànxi to convince him to alter his mind. Eventually, he agreed.

They both took a break on the dry grass after helping one other out, and Xiaowan then said, "Young master, which direction shall we go tonight to go to the mansion?" Yanxi looked at Xiaowan as if she had two heads. Frustrated by this woman, he grunted and stood up, saying, "Seems you are too blind not to notice we can't find the way easily, the only solution is to find shelter to stay until tomorrow and keep this instruction with you KEEP QUIET." Xiaowan was unable to respond and instead just stared at him as though he had gone crazy.

Chapter 9

HA HA VILLAGE

Yanxi stopped moving and stopped staring at the writing on the plank in front of them before turning to look at Xiaowan for an explanation. Xiaowan, who was relieved that God had finally heard their prayers, responded, "Wow, finally God has answered our prayer young master, this is the sign placed here that there is a village here, see check it out," while pointing at the words written on it. When Gu yanxi finally spoke, he said, "actually am a young master and this is my maid we were both lost in the forest because of our spoiled carriage and can't find the way back." Xiaowan didn't know what to say because the men are hunters anyway and she believes the two of them will be a scapegoat tonight, but her thought was ruined when Gu yanxi finally spoke. Yanxi and Xiaowan are perplexed by

the men's spontaneous laughter in place of a response.
They finally responded, saying, "Even if we want to help, we don't offer help to lairs." Gu yanxi was confused and responded, "We are not lying," but they replied, saying the most shocking thing for the two of them, "And you want me to believe that she is your maid rather than your wife uhh, I know men for a lie but say the truth and if you are not ready to say the truth am afraid we are just wasting our time lets
Can a man and woman interact at night? Okay, let's go to the village.
When they arrived, they both noticed that many people were eating, drinking, and dancing as if something significant had occurred. They exchange confused looks, and only then did Yanxi realize that he was still holding her close to him. He then released her and said, "Remember to act accordingly okay."
Since you are the one who came up with this, you should understand your

responsibilities as well, not only mine, Xiaowan said with a grin. When they arrive at the tent, the village head's wife warmly welcomes them, particularly Xiaowan, while the village head is busy presenting Yanxi to everyone. She twitches one side of her lips up and motions for him to move there more quickly.

After introductions, the village chief requests that a toast be made for Yanxi and Xiaowan. However, who is allergic to alcohol, decided to force himself to drink with the chief while also forbidding Xiaowan from doing so. Yanxi then grinned and passed out; the chief laughed at him and made a team that was not for him to rest in.

www.ingramcontent.com/pod-product-compliance
Lightning Source LLC
LaVergne TN
LVHW020537160826
845677LV00015B/4105

* 9 7 9 8 3 5 3 3 2 6 8 3 0 *